LET'S GIVE TIME SOME TIME

Shardha Jain

ISBN 978-93-5667-283-3
© Shardha Jain 2022
Published in India 2022 by Pencil

A brand of
One Point Six Technologies Pvt. Ltd.
123, Building J2, Shram Seva Premises,
Wadala Truck Terminal, Wadala (E)
Mumbai 400037, Maharashtra, INDIA
E connect@thepencilapp.com
W www.thepencilapp.com

DISCLAIMER: *The opinions expressed in this book are those of the authors and do not purport to reflect the views of the Publisher.*

Author biography

A nature lover, bibliophile that has lot to say but this practical world just don't get her. A Chemistry teacher by profession but writer by chance, may be being introvert. A native of holy city, Rishikesh and a strong believer of truth and honesty.

She has been co-author of many anthologies. She is compiler of anthology - "The Words of Instinct" and "Stupid Emotions ". "Words in Shadow" is her upcoming anthology as compiler. She is founder of "Squigglers Ink" (Insta @squigglersink), which is a group of writers and castle of emotions where Squigglers stitch their emotions and learn new writing forms & skills each day with new challenges.

Her three solo books "Into The Words", "Let's Edit life" & "Schmaltz Words" is recently published. A simple soul who just never give up and a bibliophile. Paper has more patience than people all she believe. She is Shardha Jain, who prefers to dive into words rather than ersatz worldliness.

Instagram :

@shrainquotes

CONTENTS

"Time is what we want most, but what we use worst." -William Penn 8

"Time isn't the main thing. It's the only thing." -Miles Davis 9

SHRAIN POEMS 10

    THIS MOMENT 11

    LIKE A LAMP 12

    THE NIGHT 13

    A PIECE OF ME 14

    PLACE IN BOOKS 15

    I WANT TO WRITE 16

    A PEICE OF ME 17

    HOPE 18

    P E I C E S 19

    BURNING 21

    MOON 22

    MIND 23

    WE CAN 24

    POTHOLES IN THOUGHTS 25

    TIME 26

    UNIVERSE 27

B E I N G 28

TEARS FROM THE EYES 29

BETTER NEW 30

WRITERS 31

ONE DAY 32

PAPER 33

IT'S TIME 34

A TRAVELLING POEM 35

WORDS IN SHADOW 36

EVERY DAY 37

Preface

This book is collection of poems and quotes that are out of experiences of my life. Time is really powerful from the start of life till the end, but we often fails to understand that it's the only thing that is so important and powerful. Sometimes, wait doesn't worth it. Sometimes, we are not gonna get according to expectations. We should realise that life is too short to think all the fantasy of minds & hearts.The only real thing in this unreal world is time. Sometime, it's about let it go, sometime give time to time to get good time in coming time. The book is all about some thoughts and positive thinking about ongoing daily thoughts & understanding importance of little things. I hope that readers may feel the same experiences and may derive meaningful thoughts and senses from book.

SHARDHA JAIN
(SHRAIN)

"Time is what we want most, but what we use worst." -William Penn

''Time isn't the main thing. It's the only thing.''
-Miles Davis

SHRAIN
POEMS

THIS MOMENT

Don't let the moment slip away,
To hold and keep it in every way,
Absorb the vibes of the ambience,
Feel the breathe of air presence,
Listen the lub dub of the beats,
Experience the rhythm of repeats,
The path of the falling leaves,
Making to wish out of believes,
Running breeze just making insane,
Just go with the flow like hurricane,
Vapours of water making it cool,
Getting clearity out of whiropool,
Sky seems challenging the confidence,
Sewing thoughts into words condense,
The trees are watching every environs,
To stand straight even with abrasions.

LIKE A LAMP

Be like a lamp with darkness
in roots and bright in ambience,
much to explore,much to hide,
much to neglect,with beams
reflectingall over screens of mind,
finding place tosearch and find,
the shine glaringhearts and minds,
with thought twinesand exploring
energyof sparkling vibes.

THE NIGHT

Diving into the night
To avoid the fight
Of mind & heart
Without enormous effort
Emptiness being so chaotic
But starry sky making hypnotic
Deep silence as companion
Telling everything as abbreviation.
Friendship of loneliness & darkness
May be for forever in emptiness

A PIECE OF ME

A piece of me,
seems missing from me,
Feeling like some deep emptiness,
that mind and heart don't agree,
Some twisted thought in compress,
or thread tangled in some web,
trying to get the end point,
The chase for the search getting ebb,
like lost courage to climb mount,
Whatever mind thinking,
something missed often to get straight trail,
keep colliding and making ping,
Maybe lost confidence like hail,
Or the regrets of mistakes,
Making clouds of overthinking,
That's making hazy flakes,
Might be neglected or accumulating.

PLACE IN BOOKS

There is a place in my books
Where I resides most of the time
Where I don't need any rhyme
To make in sink with the time
I feel a hand to hold for forever
A gentle, kind calm endeavor
I felt lost between the lines
Where I recollect my real self
Beyond commitments in my shelf
A place to smile, live and survive
To get the breathe back to alive
With wonders of innumerable minds
That makes only better future reminds
A support of friends with support
All the time telling to make efforts
To get back to life without worries
To find calm of soul without hurries

I WANT TO WRITE

When thoughts drowned blind
I want to write to fight

When words buzzed screen of mind
I want to write to fight

When vision became blurred
I want to write to fight

When the life seems lifeless bird
I want to write to fight

A PEICE OF ME

A peice of me
seems missing from me,
Feeling like some deep emptiness,
that mind and heart don't agree,
Some twisted thought in compress,
or thread tangled in some web,
trying to get the end point,
The chase for the search getting ebb,
like lost courage to climb mount,
Whatever mind thinking,
somethingmissed often to get straight trail,
keep colliding and making ping,
Maybe lost confidence like hail,
Or the regrets of mistakes,
Making clouds of overthinking,
That's making hazy flakes,
Might be neglected or accumulating.

HOPE

There's always hope in
the photons of sunlight,
the shine of bright,
the fluttering of leaves,
the eyes with believes,
the fly of birds,
the unsaid words,
the tears in emotions,
the stammering abbreviations,
the red setting sun,
the losted illusion,
the silence of darkness,
the needle of compass,
the heights of mount,
the depths uncount,
taking of diverged trails,
the field after hails,
the loneliness of isles,
the chuckle smiles,
the shadow cast,
the ways in hast,
the waisted patience,
the vibes of ambience.

PEICES

It's nothing like broken in this world,
it's ok and no okay only.
Nothing lies between these two,
as damaged things never
perform any work unless
repaired like machines.
People feel like being
stabbed and still breathing,
it's only kind of hallucinations
of mindly thoughts.
Nobody is in pieces,
it's complete as made by
the vital force of universe.
We are in pieces because
we think we are in pieces
that makes melancholy
thoughts to surge.
Our mind is the centre to
control the vibes and soul.
Ambience and audience tricks
mind by ersatz thoughts that
may or may not exist.
Happenings are certain and not
under our control, tears or smiles
can't fix the time at one place,
time keeps moving constantly.

So, it's better to be prepare as
complete rather than in pieces
to pace with time.

BURNING

Burning doesn't means the end,
the flames keeps sigh for
inflammable thing that
ignitesthe process.
It meant for the change,
that completely not visible t
o just human eyes. It ignites
the spirit tonotice the fire.
That fire can killthe soul or
give life to it.
Only the attraction of energy
takes the flame to it's path.
The heat and light is proof
of being alive.
The time followsto the end
but after becominga lesson.

MOON

The moon is writing
from all the noise of day,
with the tides of shores of bay,
to regain the lost things,
to remind that broken strings,
to embrace the loneliness,
beyond the circle of timeliness.

MIND

Mind always knows
where to settle thoughts,
where to break illusions,
where to find corners to hide,
where to heal the soul,
where to fill the life pothole,
where ideas comes from,
where not to get drown,
where think beyond emotionalism.

WE CAN

What we can only do
is to move forward
without thinking to recreate past things
We can only fix them
with new thoughts better than before
Accepting that things are done
and its time to let it goas holding for much
can affect worse than before
Its like becoming an obstacle
in the path of something
that can be more better if explored
Some things need more time,
some less
it depends on degree of damage
we have done to compromise our self
for this worldliness
rather than acceptance and experience.

POTHOLES IN THOUGHTS

Potholes in thoughts lane
tend to wake up to
check the reality status.
Thoughts make us their slaves.
We tend to guide by uncountable
thoughts going in brain,
with no control.
But there's always gaps
everywhere, that makes
the air & light to peep into.
That's the potholes in thoughts,
that jolt us to wake the
self beyond imaginations.

TIME

Nobody can control
the direction of time,
when we can't choose rhyme,
the river of life,
in everyday routine rife,
decision of destiny,
to make as euphony,
thousands of thoughts,
some sublime, some in droughts.

UNIVERSE

Looking into the
eyes of universe,
collecting breathe of soul
to ignite the thoughts in silence.
To put some oxygen to the self,
being tarnished due to
ignorance with time.
Making stars as companion
of thinking to find
the comets of time,
clearing the doubts of presence.
Some clouds came to give roof
to imaginations and emerging
thoughts into air.
Moon too appreciating
the ambience with smile
on its face,
like telling stories of being
strongwith its soulmate, loneliness.

BEING

Being sun needs burning too
Being feather needs lightness too
Being moon needs coolness too
Being birds needs balance too
Being air needs mixture too
Being fire needs energy too
Being storm needs speed too
Being rain needs silence too
Being mountain needs strength too
Being ice needs temperature too
Being water needs coldness too
Being human needs humanity too

TEARS FROM THE EYES

Eyes seems to see beyond horizon
Everything that's written in abbreviation
Just a little courage to lost in depth
Without doing the calculations of math

Eyes being an ocean of feelings
That feel more than heartly things
When mind can't hold the moment
And nothing would help being violent

Tears came to rescue the emotions
With infinite words of many notions
Clearing the confusion of heart and mind
When being fake is killing & unkind

Heart often chases the butterfly
And doesn't bother if gets deny
Tears are the precious waters of ocean
That wants to know certain question
They holds the waves on the shore
Thoughts and talks that are just pure
Innocence of simplicity with no meaning
Just need a heart who knows reading

BETTER NEW

New version is the need of time
to get mind and soul rhyme
It's not getting some new factor
Or finding some new anchor

To know the stress of dead past
On the sky of present today
It's must to follow some fresh trail
Of soul and heart without delay

Change is the concept of time
Nothing remains same
Not he, she, you or mine
Standing kills life of moments

Same paths never leads to somewhere
Rather takes to dead end trails
That accumulates regrets and sadness
So better to analyse and become new page

To accelerate the beats of heart and mind
To shower soul with happiness and kind

WRITERS

Writers are those people who
want to hide behind the words and lines,
trying to express in complex,
to say all the hidden letters to mind,
to pour down all the grudges,
loneliness, love and hatred,
finding the calm in the patience of paper,
holding tears in eyes of ink,
Just to save the dying soul.

ONE DAY

Wait for the day,
when sun willreally shine
to light up every dark corner,
shadowed thoughts and time.
When silence will go away with the light,
shadows fail to form impressions
due to their inability to see.
When air will content
the breathe and life.
When time will tell
it's seconds
to think before moving.

May be one day,
this all will end to infinity,
when nothing matters.

PAPER

Paper has more patience
than anyone
in this whole world,
it accept as it is.
It feels the touch of memories,
scars, mistakes,hopes,
pains,unsaid emotions.

It refresh the moments
and makes
the writer alive again.

IT'S TIME

It's Time to look back past
to learn unlearn
to unhide
all hidden nerves
to get rid
of unbearable pain
to follow the butterfly
to stop chasing mirages
to stop finding destination
to think about overthinking
unthinking all hurts
disappointments
grudges, chaos of minds
to hold moments
to heal the soul
to find the right things
to get lost in world of self
to smile with the mirror person
to become the new version

A TRAVELLING POEM

Just in one lane or another
Nothing seems to be ending
Roads are interconnected & whirled
My thoughts make me wanderer
in the world of my thinking & imagination

No purpose with might be overthinking often
Nothing seems to be still
Sometimes unconscious out of reality
To get some mirage in desert of dreams

My mind makes me to travel anywhere
but sometimes drowning
Suffocating, hesitating
in the land of imagination
without watering thoughts

WORDS IN SHADOW

Millions of thoughts in whirl
Colliding on the walls of mind
With hidden meanings in the curl
Flowing without halt in wind
In the struggle of "If I can"
Ending only at "Let it go"
Trapped in ersatz world's scan
Some in doubts, shy or ego
Carrying immense purity of thoughts
As random are always unadulterated
Ultimately overthinking making droughts
Finally mind & the heart collaborated
In the search of being accepted
Thousands words get silenced
Maybe once tried in abbreviated
Lost hope in fear of inexperienced
But still alive in the instinct shadow
Better to express voiceless thoughts
Than just hiding alone & swallow
We are alive not programmed robots
Everything becomes unclear when agitated
Settling makes better view of vision
Holding thoughtful words makes palpitated
Let them flow without appreciation

EVERY DAY

Every day expect
more serenity,
more positivity,
more kind self,
more forgiveness,
more reality,
more spirituality,
more sense,
more calmness

www.ingramcontent.com/pod-product-compliance
Lightning Source LLC
LaVergne TN
LVHW041806190726
843493LV00008B/2810